Loop Speak™: The Interest & Situation Framework

Published by D Publishing Group™ Powered by D Investment Enterprise LLC

Published by D Publishing Group™ Powered by D Investment Enterprise LLC

Disclaimer of Liability and Professional Advice:

The information provided in this book is for educational and informational purposes only and is not intended as formal legal, financial, or professional business advice. While every effort has been made to ensure the accuracy and effectiveness of the Loop Speak™ framework, the publisher and author assume no responsibility for errors, omissions, or contrary interpretations of the subject matter herein.

The success of the strategies discussed depends heavily on the reader's own execution, market conditions, and individual circumstances. By reading this document, you acknowledge that Said by Devon, D Publishing Group™, and D Investment Enterprise LLC are not liable for any direct or indirect losses, damages, or disruptions to business resulting from the application of this material.

Table of Contents

Published by D Publishing Group™ Powered by D Investment Enterprise LLC

The Interest Factor

1

Designing the Pull

Let's start with the first driver: interest. Interest is the force that pulls you in through pure curiosity, eliminating the need for anyone to chase you down. In the Loop Speak™ framework, we do not view interest as a passive emotion. We view it as a structural mechanism.

When a piece of information is directly connected to your identity, your goals, or your personal status, you actively want to learn it. The human brain is a highly efficient engine; it constantly runs a subconscious Return on Investment (ROI) calculation on where to direct its attention. If the information does not elevate the person's status, solve a current frustration, or align with how they view themselves, the brain simply filters it out as noise.

You do not have to be convinced to pay attention to something you inherently value. Think about it logically: nobody has to force a person who loves cars to sit down and read about engines. They will voluntarily binge the information. That is the definition of pure, interest-driven learning.

The Identity Connection

Most educators, leaders, and marketers fail because they try to teach the *mechanics* of a subject before establishing the *identity* connection. They try to teach the engine without verifying if the person actually loves the car.

Consider a standard corporate financial wellness seminar. If you try to teach "budgeting and frugality," the audience will tune out. Why? Because the identity of a "budgeter" feels restrictive and lacking in power. There is no status elevation.

However, if you take the exact same mathematical principles and rebrand the lesson as "how to leverage cash flow to buy back your time and build structural independence," you instantly trigger interest. The audience leans in. You have not changed the math; you have simply attached the information to an identity they desperately want to achieve.

The Secret Over The Lesson

To engineer momentum, your communication must stop sounding like a mandate and start sounding like a competitive advantage. People resent being taught, but they love discovering secrets that give them leverage.

When you frame your knowledge as an exclusive operational framework rather than a standard lesson, you activate the "pull." You eliminate the friction of instruction because the audience is too busy trying to extract the value for their own benefit.

Action Prompt: Designing the Pull

- What core identity or deep-seated goal does your target audience hold?currently facing right now?

- How can you reframe your core message so it feels like a secret they want to discover, rather than a lesson they have to learn?

*'Gold measures fear.
The Dinar measures faith.
The Dollar measures
dependence.'*

— Devon Mclarty®, The Financial Engine™

Published by D Publishing Group™
Powered by D Investment Enterprise LLC

The Situation Factor

2

The Catalyst of Urgency

If Interest is the force that pulls you in, the Situation is the force that pushes you forward.

We now move to the other side of the spectrum: situation-driven learning. This occurs when the world physically, professionally, or financially backs you into a corner, and you have absolutely no choice but to adapt.

When a person is backed into a corner, the brain's priority shifts entirely. It bypasses the luxury of curiosity and enters pure crisis management. You are not acquiring knowledge because you want to, but because you simply cannot afford not to.

The Psychology of the Corner

Think about how you operate under pressure. Maybe you suddenly lost your job and had to figure out how to freelance overnight. Maybe an unexpected bill hit, and you had to learn how to negotiate a payment plan within 24 hours.

In these moments, learning speed accelerates exponentially. Why? Because the cost of ignorance is immediate and painful. This is learning under extreme pressure.

To engineer momentum in your own business or communication, you must understand the three primary vectors of situational pressure your audience faces:

1. **Financial Urgency:** The immediate threat of losing capital or the sudden requirement to generate it. (e.g., An impending tax deadline or a sudden rent increase).
2. **Structural Urgency:** The rules of their industry or environment have suddenly changed, and their current skills are instantly obsolete. (e.g., A new technology disrupting their job security).
3. **Time Urgency:** A rapidly closing window of opportunity that will not open again.

Positioning the Escape Route

The biggest mistake creators make when their audience is under pressure is trying to sell them a "better philosophy."

If your audience is trapped in a burning building, you do not sell them a book on fire safety protocols; you sell them the map to the exit door. Your framework, your product, or your communication must be positioned as the immediate, structural escape route. You must clearly articulate exactly how your solution relieves the pressure of their current situation faster than they could figure it out on their own.

Action Prompt: Designing the Catalyst

- Identify the "Corner": What is the specific external pressure, crisis, or "corner" your target audience is currently facing right now?

____

____

____

____

- Categorize the Pressure: Is their urgency Financial, Structural, or Time-based? Describe how it specifically impacts their daily life.

____

____

____

____

- The Escape Route: How does your product, service, or framework serve as the immediate escape route from that exact pressure? (Be structural, not emotional).

____

____

____

____

*'Gold measures fear.
The Dinar measures faith.
The Dollar measures
dependence.'*

— Devon Mclarty®, The Financial Engine™

Published by D Publishing Group™
Powered by D Investment Enterprise LLC

Why Most Education Fails

3

The Desert Problem

Here is the core problem with modern instruction: most schools, digital courses, and corporate training programs attempt to teach entirely outside of both interest and urgency.

They operate under the "Information Illusion"—the false belief that simply transmitting data is enough to cause a change in human behavior. It is no wonder that the information fails to stick. If there is no intrinsic desire pulling the audience in, and no external pressure pushing them forward, the human brain simply does not have a compelling reason to retain the data.

The Desert Problem

Delivering facts without context is the equivalent of giving someone a perfectly written, beautifully illustrated fishing manual in the middle of the desert.

Think about the structure of that failure. The manual itself might be flawless. The techniques inside might be highly effective. But because the person is standing in the middle of a desert, there is no water (opportunity), there is no hunger for fish (interest), and there is absolutely no hook.

The information is factually correct, but contextually worthless.

This is exactly what happens when you try to teach a team, a client, or a student without first anchoring the lesson to their current reality. You are handing them a solution to a problem they do not currently feel. They will drop the manual and keep walking.

Engineering Relevance

If you want your information to stick, you must stop focusing solely on the quality of your "manual" and start engineering the environment. You must either move your audience to the water, or make them acutely aware of their hunger, *before* you hand them the instructions.

In the Loop Speak™ framework, relevance is not a buzzword; it is a structural requirement. You must prove to your audience that the information you hold is the exact tool they need to survive or dominate the specific environment they are currently standing in.

Action Prompt: Auditing the Desert

- Audit your current curriculum, sales pitch, or leadership style: Where are you currently delivering facts, data, or instructions without first establishing

- Identify the "Desert": Look at your audience's current environment. Why does your current "manual" feel useless or irrelevant to their immediate daily reality?

- Inject the Hook: How can you manufacture immediate relevance? What specific problem can you highlight to make them *ask* for the manual before you give it to them?

'Gold measures fear.
The Dinar measures faith.
The Dollar measures
dependence.'

— Devon Mclarty®, The Financial Engine™

Published by D Publishing Group™
Powered by D Investment Enterprise LLC

The Financial Engine™ Approach

4

Merging Intrinsic Desire and External Pressure

Inside The Financial Engine™, we refuse to let information fall flat. We understand that relying on just one driver—either purely interest or purely situation—leaves your strategy vulnerable.

If you rely only on interest, your audience might love the idea but lack the urgency to execute it *today*. If you rely only on the situation, you create stress and resentment; they act out of fear, but they will abandon the structure the second the pressure lifts.

To build permanent momentum, we purposefully merge both of these forces together. This is the core architecture of Loop Speak™.

The Unbreakable Loop

First, we create an emotional hook so that you actively desire the knowledge. We align the information directly with your highest aspirations—status, wealth, freedom, or identity. This creates the "Pull."

Then, we clearly show you the cost of not acting so that you immediately feel the urgency of the situation. We reveal the structural consequence of staying stagnant. This creates the "Push."

When you are simultaneously pulled forward by your own desires and pushed forward by external reality, you enter an unbreakable loop. That combined pressure is exactly why our Interest + Situation Learning Framework is so highly effective—it is engineered to make people not just hear your words, but physically move and take action.

The Approach in Action: The Manager's Dilemma

Let's look at a structural example. Imagine a sales manager trying to get their team to adopt a complex new tracking software.

- **The Traditional Way (Failure):** The manager sends an email saying, "This new software is mandatory. Here is the manual. Please read it." *(The Desert Problem: No hook, no urgency).*

- **The Interest Approach (Weak):** "This new software will make the company more efficient and help us reach our Q4 goals!" *(The team doesn't care about the company's efficiency; they care about their own).*

- **The Financial Engine™ Approach (The Loop):** The manager says, "This new software automatically flags high-net-worth leads so you can close faster and maximize your commission checks *(The Interest/Pull)*. However, the old system is being permanently shut down on Friday at 5:00 PM, and any leads not transferred will be lost to the house *(The Situation/Push)*."

The team doesn't just read the manual; they devour it. They actively seek out the training because the manager engineered an environment where adopting the new structure was the only logical way to protect their identity as top earners and escape the impending deadline.

Action Prompt: Engineering the Merge

- The Pull (Interest): Look at the core message or product you are trying to deliver. What is the emotional hook that will make your audience *want* to adopt it?

____
____
____
____

- The Push (Situation): What is the impending deadline, market shift, or structural consequence you can highlight to make them realize they must act *now*?

____
____
____
____

- The Merge: Write a single, concise sentence that combines both forces. (e.g., "If you learn this [Interest], you will gain [Status], but if you wait until [Date/ Event], you will lose [Consequence]").

____
____
____
____

'Gold measures fear.
The Dinar measures faith.
The Dollar measures dependence.'

— Devon Mclarty®, The Financial Engine™

Published by D Publishing Group™
Powered by D Investment Enterprise LLC

The Framework in Action

5

Designing the Loop (Workbook)

To build this into your own intellectual property, you cannot just understand the theory. You must execute the blueprint. This section is designed to transform your abstract ideas into a tangible, structural asset.

For each of the following five steps, you will define the exact mechanics of your next product launch, piece of content, or team directive. Do not skip a step. In this system, nothing is random.

Step 1: Identify the Hook (The Pull)

Your audience is moving fast. To stop them, you cannot just yell louder; you must speak directly to their identity. The hook is not a clever marketing phrase—it is the structural anchor that connects your information to their deepest desires.

- **The Amateur Approach:** "Here is a 5-step guide to saving money."
- **The Architect Approach:** "How to structurally buy back your time and permanently escape the W-2 cycle."

____

____

____

Execution Prompt:

What is the core identity, status, or ultimate freedom your audience is desperately trying to achieve?

____

____

____

____

How can you reframe your current offering so that it directly promises that exact identity or status?

____

____

____

____

Step 2: Create the Tension (The Push)

Once they are hooked by their own desires, you must introduce the corner. If there is no cost to waiting, they will wait forever. You must make them viscerally feel the structural consequence of not acting today.

- **The Amateur Approach:** "You should really buy this before the price goes up."
- **The Architect Approach:** "The market is shifting on the 1st of the month. If your infrastructure is not updated by then, your competitors will absorb your market share."

Execution Prompt:

What is the specific external pressure, impending deadline, or market threat your audience is currently ignoring?

How can you reframe your current offering so that it directly promises that exact identity or status?

Step 3: Show the Path (The Frictionless Step)

You have created immense pressure and desire. If you ask them to do something complicated right now, they will freeze. Overwhelm kills momentum. You must give them the smallest, most frictionless next step possible to cross the threshold.

- **The Amateur Approach:** "Click here to buy my massive 40-hour masterclass and change your life!"
- **The Architect Approach:** "Download this single, 1-page PDF checklist to audit your current vulnerability right now."

Execution Prompt:

What is the specific external pressure, impending deadline, or market threat your audience is currently ignoring?

How can you reframe your current offering so that it directly promises that exact identity or status?

Step 4: Deliver the Win (The Proof Engine)

When they take that frictionless step, you must immediately validate their decision. You must deliver a quick, highly visible result. This builds structural trust and proves that your framework actually functions.

- **The Amateur Approach:** Sending a welcome email that says, "Thanks for downloading, read this tomorrow!"
- **The Architect Approach:** The checklist instantly reveals a critical error they are making, allowing them to fix it and save $100 in five minutes.

____

____

____

Execution Prompt:

What is the specific, measurable "Micro-Win" you will deliver to them within the first 10 minutes of them engaging with your product?

____

____

____

How will you make sure they physically notice and acknowledge that win?

____

____

____

Step 5: Loop the Cycle (Permanent

A single win is a transaction. A looped cycle is a business. Once you deliver the first win, you must immediately use that momentum to introduce the next hook and the next situation. This transforms a one-time student into a permanent consumer of your intellectual property.

- **The Amateur Approach:** "Hope you liked the checklist! See you later."
- **The Architect Approach:** "You just fixed your vulnerability and saved $100. But that $100 is losing value to inflation daily. Here is the framework to invest it before the market closes on Friday."

Execution Prompt:

How does the "Micro-Win" from Step 4 naturally create a brand new problem or desire for your audience?

What is the next "Hook" and "Tension" you will introduce to pull them into your next, higher-tier product or lesson?

Conclusion: The Call to Action

So whether you are teaching finance, building a global brand, or just trying to get your team to actually listen to you... you must stop thinking that providing information alone is enough.

You have to hook them with interest. You must press them with the situation. When you do that, you will watch the learning stick exactly like it was designed to.

This is Loop Speak™, powered by D Investment Enterprise. And remember – inside this system, nothing is ever random. Every plan is a blueprint... waiting for a blue note.

About the Author: Devon

Devon is the architect behind The Financial Engine™ and the creator of the Loop Speak™ communication framework. Driven by the philosophy that education must provoke action, Devon specializes in transforming abstract concepts into actionable Structural Intelligence.

Operating under the belief that "in this system, nothing is random," Devon designs strategies where every plan serves as a blueprint waiting for a blue note. Through D Investment Enterprise, Devon builds systems that engineer momentum, force adaptation, and turn ideas into powerful, lasting intellectual property.

The Audio Engine: Said by Devon

The Frequency of the Framework

You now possess the structural blueprint of Loop Speak™. You understand the mechanics of desire, the catalyst of pressure, and how to engineer unbreakable momentum in the physical world.

But the Financial Engine™ does not solely operate in written text. It operates in frequency.

"Said by Devon" is the auditory extension of this exact philosophy. It is the "Blue Note" translated into sound. The same structural intensity, authority, and architecture that powers this framework has been engineered into our official music catalog.

Do not just read the blueprint. Experience the audio architecture.

SCAN TO ENTER THE SAID BY DEVON ECOSYSTEM

Published by D Publishing Group™ Powered by D Investment Enterprise LLC

Licensing & Permissions:

Published by D Publishing Group™
[DPGnetwork83@gmail.com]

First Edition: 2026 Printed in the United States of America.

Published by D Publishing Group™

Powered by D Investment Enterprise LLC

ISBN: 979-8-9950444-6-8

Printed in the United States of America

www.ingramcontent.com/pod-product-compliance
Lightning Source LLC
LaVergne TN
LVHW051136210926
848482LV00006B/334

* 9 7 9 8 9 9 5 0 4 4 4 6 8 *